THE
NBA
A HISTORY OF HOOPS

Published by Creative Education
P.O. Box 227, Mankato, Minnesota 56002
Creative Education is an imprint of The Creative Company
www.thecreativecompany.us

Design and production by Christine Vanderbeek
Art direction by Rita Marshall

Printed by Corporate Graphics in the United States of America

Photographs by Corbis (Steve Lipofsky), Dreamstime (Munktcu), Getty Images
(Brian Babineau/NBAE, Steve Babineau/NBAE, Andrew D. Bernstein/NBAE,
Nathaniel S. Butler/NBAE, Kevin C. Cox, Tim Defrisco, Steve Dunwell, Ron
Hoskins/NBAE, Walter Iooss Jr./NBAE, Walter Iooss Jr./Sports Illustrated,
NBAP/NBAE, Manny Millan/Sports Illustrated, Dick Raphael/NBAE, Dick
Raphael/Sports Illustrated, SM/AIUEO), iStockphoto (Brandon Laufenberg)

Library of Congress Cataloging-in-Publication Data
Caffrey, Scott.
The story of the Boston Celtics / by Scott Caffrey.
p. cm. — (The NBA: a history of hoops)
Includes index.
Summary: The history of the Boston Celtics professional basketball
team from its start in 1946 to today, spotlighting the franchise's
greatest players and reliving its most dramatic moments.
ISBN 978-1-58341-937-3
1. Boston Celtics (Basketball team)—Juvenile literature. 2. Boston Celtics
(Basketball team)—History. 3. Basketball—History. I. Title. II. Series.
GV885.52.B67 C35 2010   796.323'640974461—dc22   2009034777

CPSIA: 120109 PO1093

First Edition
2 4 6 8 9 7 5 3 1

Page 3: Guard Dennis Johnson (left) and forward Larry Bird
Pages 4–5: Championship banners in Boston Garden

THE STORY OF THE

BOSTON
CELTICS

SCOTT CAFFREY

CREATIVE C EDUCATION

CONTENTS

CHAPTER ONE

THE CELTICS ARE BORN

Boston, Massachusetts, is one of America's oldest and most historically rich cities. Puritans seeking to escape persecution in Europe settled there in 1630. Five years later, America's first public school was founded, and in 1636, Harvard College became America's first institution of higher learning. On December 16, 1773, American colonists staged the Boston Tea Party, a protest that sparked the American Revolution. Today, Boston is home to some of the nation's most vital industries and influential museums.

Boston is also one of the country's biggest sports towns, home to professional teams that are some of the most successful in their respective leagues. And with 17 championships, no team has been more successful in the National Basketball Association (NBA) than the Boston Celtics. The team's first owner, Walter Brown, also managed the Boston Garden arena and observed that fellow arena owners were starting to sponsor professional teams. So in 1946, he launched the Celtics, explaining his choice of name to publicist Howie McHugh as one that made sense for the area. "The name has a great tradition," Brown said. "And besides, Boston's full of Irishmen. We'll give them green uniforms and call them Celtics."

The cultural center of the northeastern region known as "New England," Boston has both a rich history and a scenic, waterfront skyline.

RED AUERBACH'S BASKETBALL INNOVATIONS ARE STILL AFFECTING THE NBA IN POSITIVE WAYS. But during his heyday, Auerbach was one of the most disliked coaches in the sport. His habit of lighting a cigar whenever the Celtics were about to win may have been acceptable inside Boston Garden, but everywhere else, the crowds—and even his own players—felt he was rubbing defeat in opponents' faces. Yet beneath that conceited exterior, Auerbach made a point of building a harmonious team atmosphere where white and black players could comfortably work together. Considering the era in which Auerbach coached, his was a very forward-thinking attitude. "I treated [players] with respect…. I treated my players like people," he said. "I respected their intelligence. I was straight with them, and they were straight with me. I didn't lie to them, and they didn't lie to me. There was no double standard." Auerbach's prejudice-free philosophy became known as "Celtic Pride," and it can be traced all the way back to 1950, when he drafted forward Chuck Cooper, one of the first African American players in the NBA.

INTRODUCING…
RED AUERBACH

COACH, GENERAL MANAGER
CELTICS SEASONS
AS COACH 1950–66
AS GENERAL MANAGER 1967–84

The franchise began as a member of the 11-team Basketball Association of America (BAA). Since Brown possessed only limited knowledge of the game, he wanted an experienced head coach to lead his team. After missing out on his first choice, Brown turned to John "Honey" Russell, a former professional player who had molded Seton Hall University into a college powerhouse. In their first season, the Celtics achieved a 22–38 record, but even that paltry win total seemed more a result of Irish luck than talent. Although the Celtics boasted the league's third-best defense, their offense ranked dead last. Center Connie Simmons, with his average of 10.3 points per game, was the lone bright spot. The next season didn't get much better, but Russell was able to obtain 6-foot-5 Cleveland Rebels center Ed Sadowski, a player he had coached at Seton Hall. While Sadowski helped the second-year Celtics achieve a playoff berth, they lost to the Chicago Stags in the first round.

After two disappointing seasons, Russell was replaced by Alvin "Doggie" Julian in 1948. But the coaching switch made very little impact. "Things were going so bad that even my wife wanted me to get out of the business," Brown said later. Despite his wife's protest, Brown spent most of his life savings to keep the struggling franchise from bankruptcy. His ter   and vision paid off. And so did his trust in team investor Lou

Pieri, who convinced Brown to hire a brash young coach by the name of Arnold "Red" Auerbach in 1950, a year after the BAA merged with the National Basketball League (NBL) to become the NBA.

Auerbach quickly established himself as an intimidating coach who would not tolerate losing. "I don't care who it was, if one of his players stepped out of line, Red would descend on him with both feet," former St. Louis Hawks forward Bob Pettit said. "Red was different. You had to respect him, even if you didn't like him." Auerbach intimidated everyone—referees, fans, scorers, and opposing coaches—and sometimes even did so physically. He also became infamous for lighting a cigar when a win was imminent.

Auerbach soon reshaped his roster with talented young players such as point guard Bob Cousy, guard Bill Sharman, and forward Chuck Cooper. A flashy, 6-foot-1 spitfire, Cousy made the biggest impact. His sleight-of-hand passes sometimes fooled not only his opponents but his teammates as well. "Cousy was the catalyst for our team," said Auerbach. "He drove the guys to play their best."

COURTSIDE STORIES

THE FIRST CELTIC

Walter Brown (with ball) and Celtics players in 1960.

WALTER BROWN TOOK OVER AS GENERAL MANAGER OF THE BOSTON GARDEN AFTER HIS FATHER GEORGE, THE ARENA'S FIRST GENERAL MANAGER, PASSED AWAY IN 1939. Brown quickly rose through the executive ranks, and in 1941, he was promoted to Garden president. Brown was so successful at promoting sports that he would go on to earn the title of "Boston's greatest sportsman," and according to sports historian Richard A. Johnson, it was well deserved: "[Brown] was simply a model of modesty, competence, and gentility in a profession filled with self-promotion, greed, and envy." Brown launched the Celtics in 1946 as a way to fill seats when the Boston Bruins professional hockey team was on the road. "You can't treat this like a straight business," Brown said. "It is too much of a business to be a sport and too much of a sport to be a business." Brown knew little about basketball, so he hired the ultimate architect, Red Auerbach, to put together a team. Auerbach gave Brown seven NBA titles, including six straight, before the beloved owner passed away in 1964.

CHAPTER TWO

THE UNBEATABLE CHAMPIONS

From 1950 to 1956, the Celtics made the playoffs every year. But Auerbach knew the kind of players he needed to win a championship, and he got them during the 1956 NBA Draft. He selected local College of the Holy Cross star forward Tom Heinsohn and University of San Francisco guard K. C. Jones. Then he orchestrated a draft-day trade with the St. Louis Hawks for Jones's teammate, center Bill Russell.

Boston bolted to a 13–3 start in 1956–57, even without Russell, who arrived in December after participating in the Olympics as part of the gold-medal-winning United States team. Russell's league-leading rebounding average (19.6 boards per night) boosted Boston to a 44–28 record. The Celtics went on to sweep the Syracuse Nationals in the Eastern Division finals and then met the Hawks in the NBA Finals. The deciding Game 7 was a classic, as the teams battled through two overtime periods before Boston finally pulled out a 125–123 victory to claim its first NBA championship. "Winning your first championship is always the hardest," Auerbach said.

Tom Heinsohn exceeded expectations in his first NBA season, netting 16.2 points per game to earn the 1957 Rookie of the Year award.

Little did the coach know that Boston's second attempt the following season would be even more difficult. In Game 3 of the 1958 Finals against St. Louis, Russell sprained his ankle, and Boston lost 111–108. But the team rallied around veteran backup center Arnie Risen in Game 4 to achieve a 109–98 victory. And although Russell taped his ankle and gave a valiant effort in Game 6, the Hawks recovered to win the game and championship by one point, 110–109. Dismayed by the defeat, Cousy later said, "Everyone knows how great Russell was and what he meant to us. He was severely hampered by that ankle. All I know is that without question, the Hawks were the second-best team that year."

Compelled to prove themselves after the bitter loss, the vengeful Celtics went on a rampage the following season and bombarded the Minneapolis Lakers in a four-game 1959 Finals sweep to take home their second title. Auerbach's continued preaching of fundamentals and emphasis on physical conditioning went a long way toward ensuring Boston's success. "By opening night, we were the

ONCE, WHEN BOB COUSY WAS 13 YEARS OLD, HE CLIMBED TO THE TOP OF A TREE, SLIPPED, CRASHED ONTO A SIDEWALK, AND BROKE HIS RIGHT ARM—HIS SHOOTING ARM. Cousy wondered if he would ever play basketball again. But since he was so addicted to the sport, he simply taught himself how to shoot left-handed and continued to practice. Cousy was only an average high school player, but he worked exhaustively on all aspects of his game, at any time of day, whatever the weather. He was so dedicated that he made himself a promise to become a college All-American some day. He not only achieved that goal three times over at Massachusetts' College of the Holy Cross, but he went on to greater heights as an NBA star. Cousy, one of the NBA's rare lefties, led the league in assists for 8 straight seasons, played in 13 consecutive All-Star Games, and won 1 league Most Valuable Player (MVP) award. As coach Red Auerbach once famously proclaimed, "I've got news for you. There ain't nobody as good as Cooz. There never was."

INTRODUCING...

BILL RUSSELL

POSITION CENTER
HEIGHT 6-FOOT-10
CELTICS SEASONS
AS PLAYER 1956–69
AS PLAYER / COACH 1966–69

OF ALL THE AMAZING ACCOMPLISHMENTS BILL RUSSELL ACHIEVED IN HIS CELTICS CAREER, PERHAPS HIS GREATEST WAS MAKING DEFENSE A RESPECTABLE PART OF THE GAME. Red Auerbach had never seen Russell play in college, yet he traded for him in 1956 based on his reputation alone. Russell's aggressive style of play completely bewildered his opponents. With his sharp elbows, he dished out punishment as well as he absorbed it. But more than anything, he used his intelligence to exploit the psychological aspects of the game, intimidating opponents by getting inside their heads. Russell figured if he could prevent a player from driving the lane, he had already won a major battle. He was so dominant that even he became aware of the whispers going around the league, joking in 1961 that, "They still call this club four shooters and Bill Russell." But nothing was further from the truth. Russell was a team player who knew that the Celtics' success rested with all five players on the court working together. It was a philosophy he put into action to help Boston win 11 NBA titles (2 as player/coach) during his tenure.

best-conditioned team in the league," All-Star guard Bill Sharman remembered. "So every year, he'd get us off to a great start, and that would bolster our confidence." The 1959–60 season was a prime example as Boston raced to a 30–4 start. Finishing with a 59–16 record, the team went on to capture its third championship in four seasons.

With guard Sam Jones and forward Tom "Satch" Sanders adding extra punch, the Celtics remained a virtually unstoppable force and racked up seven consecutive league championships from 1960 to 1966. In the midst of that charmed run, the dominant Russell won the NBA's MVP award four times, but the Celtics also experienced loss. In 1964, team owner Walter Brown passed away, and future Hall of Fame forward Frank Ramsey retired, yet Boston continued to roll, clinching league titles again in 1965 and 1966.

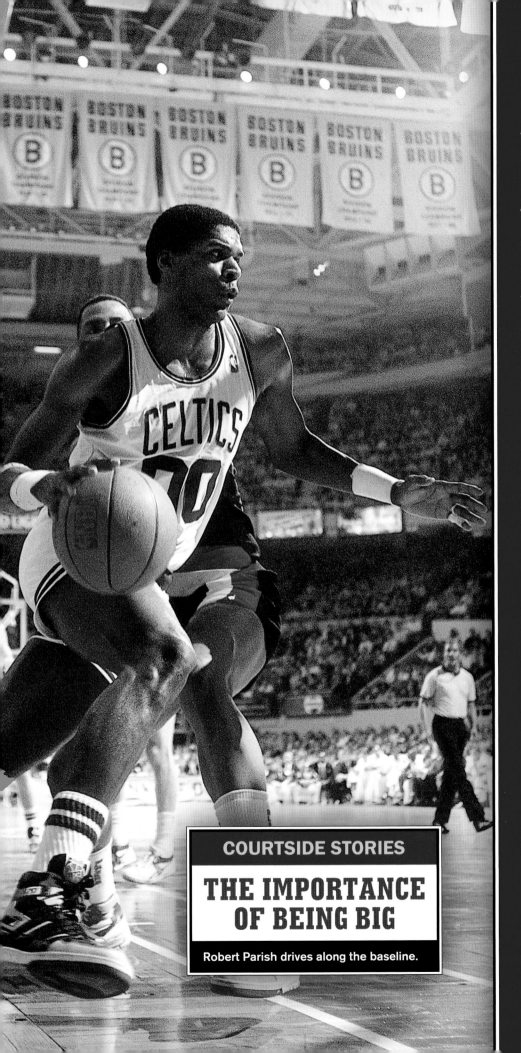

COURTSIDE STORIES

THE IMPORTANCE OF BEING BIG

Robert Parish drives along the baseline.

AMONG THE MANY INNOVATIVE PHILOSOPHIES THAT CELTICS COACH RED AUERBACH DEVELOPED WAS THE IMPORTANCE OF OBTAINING DOMINANT BIG MEN, AND HE PROVED IT TIME AND AGAIN. The first such trade, in 1956, was considered a blockbuster. Auerbach sent two players (center Ed Macauley and forward Cliff Hagan) to the St. Louis Hawks for the Hawks' top draft pick, center Bill Russell (6-foot-10). That trade helped the Celtics develop into the most dominant franchise in NBA history. Then, in 1980, Auerbach dealt two high draft picks to the Golden State Warriors for veteran center Robert Parish (seven feet) and the third pick overall. Auerbach spun that pick into forward Kevin McHale (6-foot-10), thereby creating a stalwart frontcourt for the next decade. Finally, 27 years later, general manager Danny Ainge used the Auerbach principle to pry forward Kevin Garnett (6-foot-11) away from the Minnesota Timberwolves, courtesy of Minnesota's team president, Kevin McHale. The very next season, the Celtics won the franchise's 17th championship. Like Russell, Parish, and McHale, Garnett proved once again that talented big men lead to titles.

In Game 7 of the 1965 Eastern Division finals, forward and team captain John Havlicek made a memorable steal in the waning seconds to propel Boston past the Philadelphia 76ers and toward another title. In 1966, the Celtics followed the exact same road—beating the 76ers in the division finals and the Los Angeles Lakers in the Finals—to win it all again. After winning his ninth title in a decade, Auerbach retired from coaching to become the team's general manager and turned to the trusted Russell as his replacement. Reluctantly, Russell accepted the dual role of player/coach, thereby becoming the first African American coach in NBA history.

In Russell's first season at the helm, Boston lost the Eastern Division finals but bounced back in 1967–68 to win the first of two consecutive league titles, bringing the franchise to a total of 11 in 13 years. "We felt we were good, we just didn't know how long we could keep it going," Havlicek later said. "We were just looking for one last gasp." And what a last gasp it was.

INTRODUCING...

JOHN HAVLICEK

POSITION FORWARD / GUARD
HEIGHT 6-FOOT-5
CELTICS SEASONS 1962–78

WHEN JOHN "HONDO" HAVLICEK ENTERED THE LEAGUE IN 1962, HE WAS KNOWN AS A DEFENSIVE SPECIALIST FOR THE 1960 COLLEGE NATIONAL CHAMPION OHIO STATE UNIVERSITY. "I realized that the most difficult player to guard is the kind of player who is always moving," Havlicek said. So once Hondo hit the court, he never stopped. "You just wind him up–click, click, click–he keeps going," laughed center Bill Russell. Teammate Bob Cousy wasn't convinced and figured Havlicek for just another "non-shooter who would probably burn himself out." But Havlicek, who played both forward and guard, proved the doubters wrong and became one of the most dangerous two-way players in league history. Hondo led Boston in scoring 10 times and in assists 6 times and was the team's captain for more than a decade. But his proudest moment came on November 20, 1977, when he played his 1,123rd pro game–more than anyone else had ever played at the time. "If there's any phase of basketball I've been identified with, it's endurance," he later said. "When I broke the old record, it meant a great deal to me."

CHAPTER THREE

A NEW DYNASTY EMERGES

When Russell retired in 1969, it seemed the Celtics' magic went with him. It was a rough beginning for new coach Tom Heinsohn, who inherited a lineup that featured veterans such as forward Don Nelson, gentle seven-foot center Hank Finkel, and forward Larry Siegfried. The team went just 34–48—Boston's first losing record in 20 years.

By 1970, many experts thought the Celtics were in for a long rebuilding period. But the experts underestimated the managerial skills of Auerbach, who installed versatile rookie Dave Cowens at center, moved Havlicek up front with the improving Nelson, and revamped the backcourt with young guards Don Chaney and Jo Jo White. Havlicek starred in his best offensive season ever, grabbing 9 boards and netting a career-high 28.9 points a game to become the league's second-leading scorer behind Milwaukee Bucks center Lew Alcindor. By the 1971–72 campaign, the Celtics were potent contenders again behind the emerging stardom of Cowens. The prized left-handed shooter became the league's premier pivot man as well as Boston's undisputed floor leader.

Fast and reliable guard Jo Jo White was a seven-time All-Star who helped carry the 1970s Celtics with his leadership and accurate jumpers.

The following season, Boston soared to a franchise-record 68 victories, and Cowens earned league MVP honors. "We play Celtics basketball," explained Havlicek. "We work hard every night, and we don't care who gets the glory. It's all about the team." As if to prove Havlicek's point, one of the season's unforeseen bright spots was the rebounding prowess of forward Paul Silas, who had been obtained from the Phoenix Suns in a trade for guard Charlie Scott. Unfortunately, the Celtics' sterling regular season was capped by postseason disappointment. For the second straight year, Boston lost the Eastern Conference finals to the New York Knicks.

Coach Heinsohn finally got an NBA championship the next season against Milwaukee, but it didn't come easily. After the teams traded victories through the first five Finals contests, Kareem Abdul-Jabbar (formerly Lew Alcindor) and guard Oscar Robertson helped Milwaukee eke out a 102–101 double-overtime win in Game 6. But in the finale, the dependable Cowens out-dueled them and led Boston to a 102–87 victory, bringing its championship count to a full dozen.

Although they amassed 60 wins in 1974–75, the Celtics were outmatched in the conference finals against the Washington Bullets. However, the 1975–76 Celtics rose to championship heights once more, winning a thrilling NBA Finals series over the Phoenix Suns. The

35-year-old Havlicek, though hobbled by a leg injury, managed to lead Boston to back-to-back victories in the first two games. After the Celtics lost the next two games at Phoenix, they also nearly lost Game 5 back at home. But they hung on during three overtime periods to outlast Phoenix 128–126. The anticlimactic Game 6 was a cakewalk in comparison, as Boston claimed its 13th championship.

Just as the Celtics stumbled at the end of the 1960s with the retirements of Auerbach and Russell, they also faltered at the end of the '70s, this time due to the retirements of Coach Heinsohn and Havlicek. Heinsohn had carved out a new spot for himself in Celtics history—one of the club's most successful but underrated players in the 1950s and '60s, he had turned into one of its coaching masterminds, compiling the second-most victories in club history, with 427. Replacement coach Tom Sanders could not fill such massive shoes, and the Celtics descended to the lower rungs of the league.

IN 1976, BOSTON MET THE PHOENIX SUNS IN AN NBA FINALS SERIES HIGHLIGHTED BY A GAME 5 THAT IS KNOWN AS THE "FABULOUS FIFTH"— ONE OF ONLY TWO NBA FINALS GAMES EVER TO GO INTO TRIPLE OVERTIME. In the waning seconds of the first overtime, Phoenix forward Curtis Perry drained four straight points to force a second overtime. With five seconds remaining in the second overtime, Perry dropped another bucket to give the Suns a 110–109 edge. Then Boston forward John Havlicek hit the apparent game-winning shot. But referee Richie Powers signaled that there were two seconds left to play. So Suns coach John MacLeod tried to get creative and called a timeout—one that Phoenix didn't have. While that infraction gave Boston guard Jo Jo White one technical foul shot and the Celtics a two-point edge, it also allowed Phoenix a final inbound pass to forward Gar Heard, who hit a miraculous shot from near midcourt to force the third overtime. That's when Celtics backup center Jim Ard became the unlikely hero, contributing eight points in the 128–126 victory. Two days later, Boston captured its lucky 13th NBA championship.

THE FABULOUS FIFTH

Dave Cowens playing defense in the 1976 Finals.

CHAPTER FOUR

THE BIG THREE

Looking to lift Boston's prospects, Auerbach found new talent through the NBA Draft. In 1977, he chose forward Cedric "Cornbread" Maxwell, and in 1978, he traded with the San Diego Clippers for point guard Nate "Tiny" Archibald. Also in 1978, Auerbach drafted forward Larry Bird from Indiana State University. Bird joined the team a year later, just after Boston had suffered its worst 2-year stretch ever—winning a total of 61 games in 1977–78 and 1978–79. Bird's savvy play helped the Celtics achieve 61 wins in just 1 marvelous resurrection season. As a result, new coach Bill Fitch won the NBA Coach of the Year award, and Bird earned Rookie of the Year honors.

In 1980, Auerbach continued his draft-day tricks and trades. He brought in workhorse center Robert "Chief" Parish from the Golden State Warriors and spent a first-round draft pick on University of Minnesota star forward Kevin McHale. The reloaded Celtics barreled to a 62–20 mark and then stormed to the NBA Finals, where "The Big Three" of Bird, Parish, and McHale overwhelmed the scrappy Houston Rockets in six games to fulfill Boston's destiny as a champion once more.

Smart, long-armed, and fundamentally sound, forward Kevin McHale (left) was a formidable interior presence for Boston for 13 seasons.

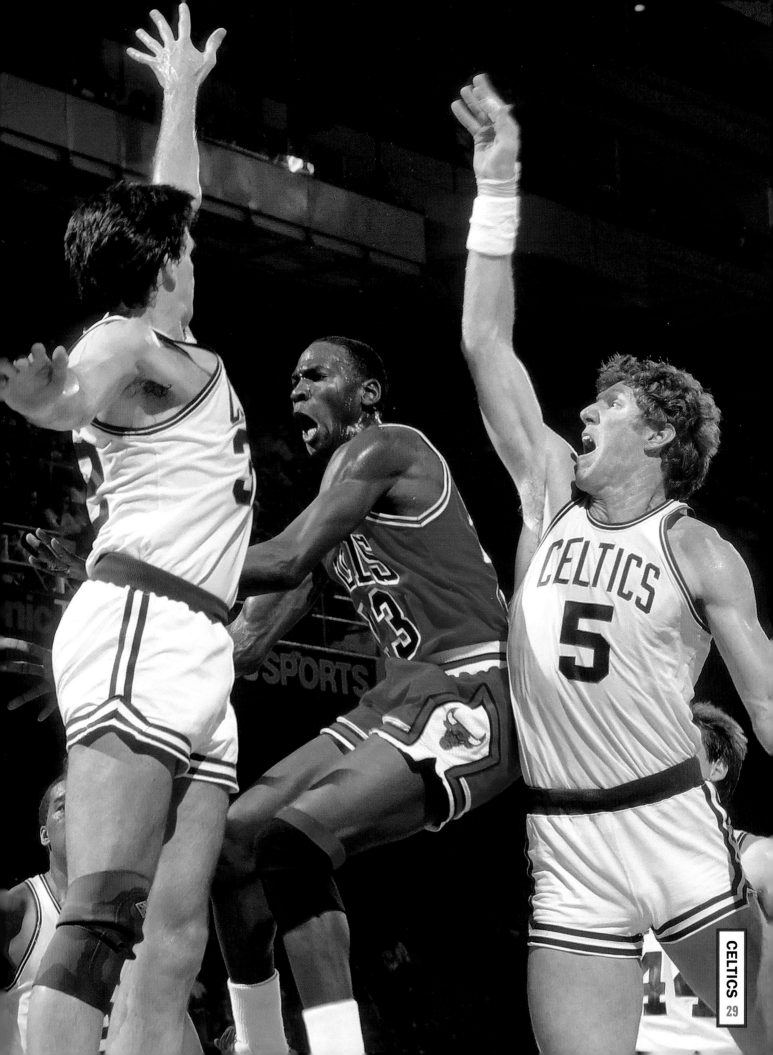

INTRODUCING...

LARRY BIRD

POSITION FORWARD
HEIGHT 6-FOOT-9
CELTICS SEASONS 1979–92

WHEN INDIANA STATE UNIVERSITY BASKETBALL COACH BOBO KING FOUND LARRY BIRD, THE FORMER HIGH SCHOOL STAR WAS DRIVING A GARBAGE TRUCK IN HIS HOMETOWN OF FRENCH LICK, INDIANA. Bird had left rival Indiana University 1974, during his first season, and King could tell that Bird still longed to play. So he convinced Bird to try again at Indiana State. Bird obliged, and in his senior year, he took the Sycamores to the 1979 college national championship game, where they lost to Magic Johnson's Michigan State University Spartans. Bird wasn't particularly gifted physically, but he practiced constantly. "I always know what's happening on the court," he said. "I know exactly what I can and cannot do." The three-time NBA MVP with the sweet shooting stroke also had nerves of steel, especially in the clutch. As the guest of honor the night the Celtics paid tribute to Bird, longtime rival Magic Johnson said, "I always told people that Larry Bird was the best all-around player that ever played the game. But more than that, he was the one player I feared and respected more than anyone else."

fter Boston was eliminated in the early rounds of the playoffs the next two years, former guard K. C. Jones was hired as head coach. Jones's championship pedigree boosted the 1983–84 Celtics back to a seven-game NBA Finals series, where they faced superstar guard Magic Johnson and the Los Angeles Lakers. Boston lost Game 1 and was on the verge of losing Game 2 when guard Gerald Henderson intercepted a crosscourt pass by Lakers forward James Worthy and tied the game with an easy layup. The Celtics went on to win that contest but lost the next. After pushing Game 4 into overtime, Boston took 2 of the final 3 games for its 15th championship.

The Big Three did not make up the whole show in Boston, though, especially not during the team's scintillating 1985–86 season. Veteran guard Dennis Johnson was a championship-caliber competitor who had already proven his big-game mettle with both the Seattle Super-Sonics and Phoenix Suns. Guard Danny Ainge brought a spark with his steady ball-handling, and veteran center Bill Walton helped hold the team together.

A valuable rebounder and scorer, Cedric "Cornbread" Maxwell played a key role in some memorable Celtics–Lakers battles of the 1980s.

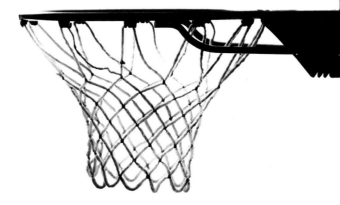

The 1985–86 Celtics lost only one game at home and were expected to go the distance. But to do so, the Celtics had to get past their old coach Bill Fitch and his Houston Rockets, which included the "Twin Towers" of forward Ralph Sampson and center Hakeem Olajuwon. As the two teams faced off in the NBA Finals, Fitch could tell that this new Celtics crew was stronger than the one he had coached. "More important than the talent," he marveled, "they were totally devoid of any players who thought personal statistics meant anything." Yet individuals such as Bird stood out, and "Larry Legend" dominated the Rockets in Game 6, recording a triple-double (double-digit tallies in 3 categories) with 29 points, 11 rebounds, and 12 assists to help claim Boston's 16th NBA championship.

Although Boston reached the Finals the next season, the Lakers won the series four games to two. Then, as with Boston's previous dynasties, the Big Three era endured a late-decade slump, this time spurred in part by successive tragedies. In 1986, the Celtics drafted standout University of Maryland forward Len Bias, who was expected to become the team's next star. But tragically, he died two days later. The next year, Boston drafted Reggie Lewis, a multitalented forward from local Northeastern University. Lewis brought youthful energy to the lineup and became the team's leader when Bird was forced to retire in 1992 due to chronic back problems. Bird finished his Hall of Fame career with averages of 24.3 points, 10 rebounds, and 6.3 assists per game. Sadly, Lewis's tenure as Bird's replacement was short-lived, as he died suddenly of a heart attack in July 1993.

COURTSIDE STORIES

TWIN TRAGEDIES

Reggie Lewis surveys the court.

JUNE 1986 SHOULD HAVE BEEN ANOTHER MAGICAL MONTH IN CELTICS HISTORY. On June 8, the team won its 16th NBA championship. Nine days later in the NBA Draft, Red Auerbach engineered a trade to land University of Maryland forward Len Bias, perhaps the most talented collegiate player available, with the second overall pick. However, June 19 seemed to be the day that the "Celtic Mystique" ran out when Bias died of a drug overdose. "It hurt our sport," said famous Duke University coach Mike Krzyzewski. "Above and beyond the loss of life, we never got to see one of those truly great ones become great." In an effort to move past the Bias tragedy, the Celtics selected Reggie Lewis from nearby Northeastern University in the next year's draft. Lewis lived up to his potential, becoming the team's captain and an All-Star. But in July 1993, during an off-season shoot-around, Lewis collapsed and died of a heart attack. These twin tragedies continued to have lasting negative repercussions on the Celtics franchise for many years afterwards.

DEE BROWN PUMPS IT UP

DEE BROWN MADE THE MOST OF HIS TIME IN BOSTON. Drafted 19th overall in 1990 from Jacksonville University, the 6-foot-1 point guard was a solid all-around passer, scorer, and defender on an unspectacular Celtics team. Although Brown never achieved superstar status, he did make the NBA's All-Rookie team and then enjoyed one star-making moment in the 1991 Slam Dunk Contest during the NBA's All-Star Game weekend. After making it to the final round, Brown tried to think of a clever idea. As he stared down at his shoes, he got one. He was wearing Reebok Pumps, the first shoes made to inflate like basketballs to provide a snug fit. Brown bent down and took a moment to pump up his shoes. He then raced to the basket, leaped, covered his eyes with his right arm, and threw down a "no-look" jam with his left hand that won the competition. The Celtics had little to get excited about for most of the '90s, but Brown did his best to rouse the Boston faithful, if only for one night.

CHAPTER FIVE

ANOTHER BIG THREE

After the shocking deaths of Bias and Lewis, the Celtics suffered a number of losing seasons in the 1990s. Looking to rebuild after moving into the new Fleet Center arena in 1995, Boston hired successful college coach Rick Pitino as its new bench leader and team president in 1997. But Pitino would never take the Celtics to a winning record. Young players such as forwards Antoine Walker and Paul Pierce showed flashes of brilliance but also struggled while adjusting to the pro game. In 2001, Jim O'Brien replaced Pitino and coached the Celtics to their first winning season (49–33) in nearly a decade.

Pierce and Walker were named team co-captains, and each averaged 20 or more points per game for 3 straight seasons from 2000–01 through 2002–03. The talented duo, along

Although capable of inside scoring, Antoine Walker preferred shooting threes, launching more than any other NBA player from 2000 to 2003.

with point guard Kenny Anderson, brought the team all the way to the 2002 Eastern Conference finals but were outmatched by Anderson's former team, the upstart New Jersey Nets. Things got worse the next season when Boston was swept by the same Nets team in the second round of the playoffs.

Just before the start of the 2003–04 season, Boston traded Walker to the Dallas Mavericks. Even without a steady partner, Pierce showed his pedigree by carrying the Celtics to the 2004 playoffs, where they were swept by the Indiana Pacers in the first round. In 2004–05, under new coach Doc Rivers, the Celtics were noticeably stronger and proved it by winning the Atlantic Division—their first division title since 1992. But once again, they lost to Indiana in the postseason.

The team had picked up high-scoring forward Al Jefferson and guard Delonte West in the 2004 NBA Draft, and in 2005, Boston nabbed 19-year-old forward Gerald Green. "These are guys that anyone in the league would kill to have," said former guard Danny Ainge, who had become Boston's executive director of basketball operations.

But Boston had found relatively little success in the 21 years since it

had won its 16th title. And after back-to-back losing seasons in 2005–06 and 2006–07, the latter of which included a franchise-record 18-game losing streak, Ainge traded with the Seattle SuperSonics for All-Star shooting guard Ray Allen. The Celtics then pulled off a historic swap, trading seven players to acquire Minnesota Timberwolves star forward Kevin Garnett. Once again, references to "The Big Three" were being thrown around Boston—this time meaning Pierce, Garnett, and Allen. "Winning a championship," Ainge said, "is now a legitimate and realistic goal."

Bolstered by talent on all sides, including youthful spark plugs such as guard Rajon Rondo and center Kendrick Perkins, the Celtics made history again by orchestrating the NBA's greatest one-year turnaround, transforming from a 24–58 disgrace into a 66–16 juggernaut in 2007–08. On Boston's way to defeating the Lakers for its 17th NBA champ-

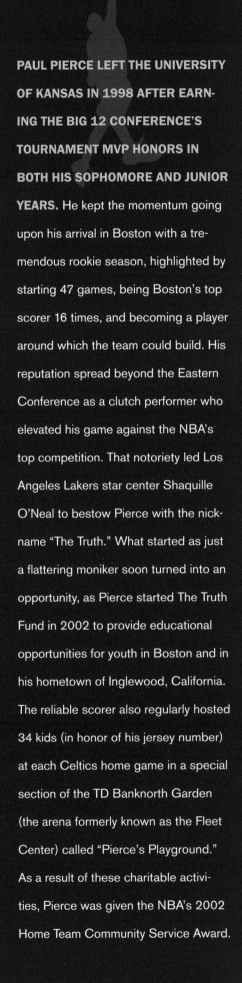

INTRODUCING...

PAUL PIERCE

POSITION FORWARD
HEIGHT 6-FOOT-6
CELTICS SEASONS 1998–PRESENT

PAUL PIERCE LEFT THE UNIVERSITY OF KANSAS IN 1998 AFTER EARNING THE BIG 12 CONFERENCE'S TOURNAMENT MVP HONORS IN BOTH HIS SOPHOMORE AND JUNIOR YEARS. He kept the momentum going upon his arrival in Boston with a tremendous rookie season, highlighted by starting 47 games, being Boston's top scorer 16 times, and becoming a player around which the team could build. His reputation spread beyond the Eastern Conference as a clutch performer who elevated his game against the NBA's top competition. That notoriety led Los Angeles Lakers star center Shaquille O'Neal to bestow Pierce with the nickname "The Truth." What started as just a flattering moniker soon turned into an opportunity, as Pierce started The Truth Fund in 2002 to provide educational opportunities for youth in Boston and in his hometown of Inglewood, California. The reliable scorer also regularly hosted 34 kids (in honor of his jersey number) at each Celtics home game in a special section of the TD Banknorth Garden (the arena formerly known as the Fleet Center) called "Pierce's Playground." As a result of these charitable activities, Pierce was given the NBA's 2002 Home Team Community Service Award.

ionship, Garnett became the first Celtics player ever to capture the NBA's Defensive Player of the Year award.

The same Boston crew remained a contender the next two seasons. After the Celtics were bounced from the second round of the 2009 playoffs, many experts thought the team's veteran stars were finally washed up. But in 2009–10, Boston surged back to the NBA Finals and very nearly captured its 18th league championship. As Rondo emerged as a true star, the Celtics took a three-games-to-two lead over the rival Lakers in the Finals, only to lose the final two contests in Los Angeles. "I told our guys after the game I couldn't have been prouder of this group…," Coach Rivers said after his team lost 83–79 in Game 7. "We're not going to be the same team next year. Guys are not going to be there, so that was tough for me. But I was just proud."

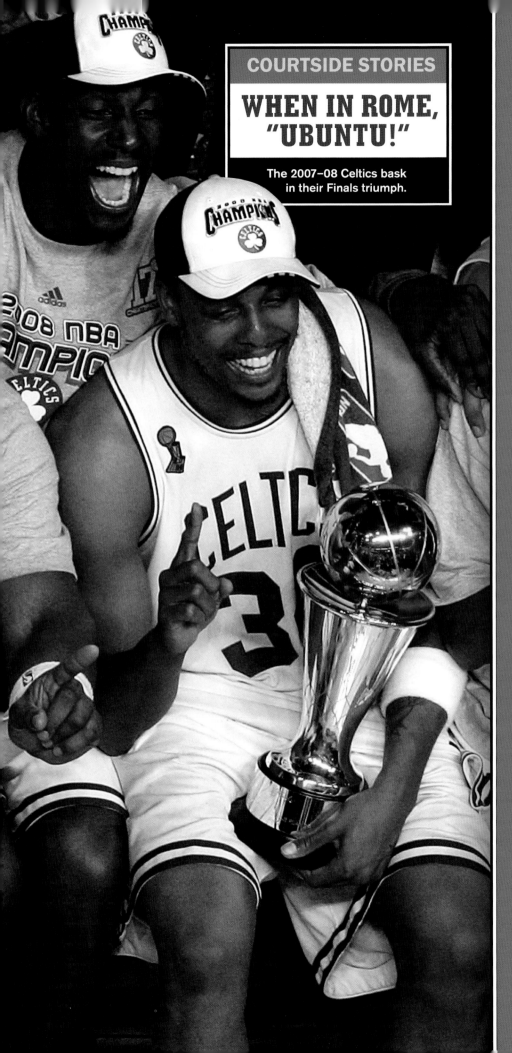

WHEN IN ROME, "UBUNTU!"

The 2007–08 Celtics bask in their Finals triumph.

"UBUNTU!" THE CELTICS SHOUTED AFTER EVERY PRACTICE DURING THEIR 2007–08 CHAMPIONSHIP SEASON. Coach Doc Rivers said he chose the chant after reading about South African leader Desmond Tutu that summer. "Ubuntu," a word from the African Bantu language, stresses collective success over individual achievement. The chant had an effect on the players, especially newly arrived superstars Kevin Garnett and Ray Allen, who went out of their way to make sure every player knew the team could succeed only if they played together. During the team's preseason exhibition trip to Rome, Italy, Paul Pierce, Rajon Rondo, and Kendrick Perkins shaved their heads to honor their new bald-headed teammates. The players often hung out together while abroad, and Garnett and Pierce even organized a team outing to watch a soccer game. "Those guys are stars, and they could have easily taken their own limos," rookie guard Gabe Pruitt said. "But they rode over with the rest of us in a bus." The team was coming together in the Red Auerbach tradition. Eight months after bonding in Rome, that Celtics crew became NBA champions.

The Boston Celtics are among the NBA's proudest franchises, and the 17 championship banners that hang from the rafters of TD Banknorth Garden are a visual reminder of their winning heritage. From the days of Cousy and Russell to those of Havlicek and Bird, the Celtics have experienced more success than most teams could dream of. With the stars in green of today—and perhaps with a little bit of Irish luck—even more championships may lie just ahead.

The Celtics enjoyed a brilliant resurgence, thanks to the acquisition of veteran stars Kevin Garnett (below) and Ray Allen (opposite).

INDEX

DISCARD
E/c